The INSIDE GUIDE

WOMEN IN U.S. HISTORY

Women in the 13 Colonies

By Therese M. Shea

Cavendish Square

Published in 2025 by Cavendish Square Publishing, LLC
2544 Clinton Street Buffalo, NY 14224

First Edition

Website: cavendishsq.com

Library of Congress Cataloging-in-Publication Data

Names: Shea, Therese, author.
Title: Women in the 13 colonies / Therese M. Shea.
Other titles: Women in the thirteen colonies
Description: New York : Cavendish Square Publishing, [2025] | Series: The inside guide: women in U.S. history | Includes index.
Identifiers: LCCN 2024023341 (print) | LCCN 2024023342 (ebook) | ISBN 9781502673039 (library binding) | ISBN 9781502673022 (paperback) | ISBN 9781502673046 (ebook)
Subjects: LCSH: Women–United States–Social conditions–17th century–Juvenile literature. | Women–United States–Social conditions–18th century–Juvenile literature. | Women–United States–History–17th century–Juvenile literature | Women–United States–History–18th century–Juvenile literature
Classification: LCC HQ1416 .S54 2025 (print) | LCC HQ1416 (ebook) | DDC 305.4097309/032–dc23/eng/20240611
LC record available at https://lccn.loc.gov/2024023341
LC ebook record available at https://lccn.loc.gov/2024023342

Editor: Therese Shea
Copyeditor: Danielle Haynes
Designer: Deanna Lepovich

The photographs in this book are used by permission and through the courtesy of: Cover AI Image Generator/Shutterstock.com; pp. 4, 24 (main), 29 (left) courtesy of the Library of Congress; p. 6 Anadolu_Dizgi/Shutterstock.com; p. 7 Interview of Samoset with the Pilgrims/Wikimedia Commons; p. 8 2nd Supply to the Virginia Colony Passenger List/Wikimedia Commons; p. 9 Christine_Kohler/iStock.com; p. 10 Land Granted by Charter to the Virginia Company in 1609/Wikimedia Commons; p. 12 William Blackstone, Commentaries on the Laws of England (1st ed, 1765, vol I, title page)/Wikimedia Commons; pp. 13, 18 Everett Collection/Shutterstock.com; p. 14 Indenturecertificate/Wikimedia Commons; p. 15 ZU_09/iStock.com; pp. 16, 20 Morphart Creation/Shutterstock.com; p. 19 Cynthia Farmer/Shutterstock.com; p. 22 cemoga/Shutterstock.com; p. 24 (inset) Michael Gordon/Shutterstock.com; p. 25 Anne Hutchinson on Trial/Wikimedia Commons; p. 26 Unidentified Artist - Phillis Wheatley - Google Art Project/Wikimedia Commons; p. 29 (right) Daniel Reiner/Shutterstock.com.

CPSIA compliance information: Batch #CWCSQ25: For further information contact Cavendish Square Publishing LLC at 1-877-980-4450.

Printed in the United States of America

CONTENTS

Jamestown in today's Virginia was the first permanent British settlement in North America, established in 1607.

Chapter One

COLONIZING THE COAST

In the 1600s and early 1700s, many European nations began establishing settlements in eastern North America. Great Britain, Spain, France, and the Netherlands were the most successful. Eventually, Britain had control of most of the East Coast. The country divided the territory into 13 large areas called colonies, which would later become the first 13 U.S. states. Women played important roles in colonial life.

From Virginia to Georgia

Britain established the first of its American colonies—Virginia—in 1624. New York followed (established in 1626), then Massachusetts (1630), Maryland (1633), Rhode Island (1636), Connecticut (1636), New Hampshire (1638), Delaware (1638), North Carolina (1653), South Carolina (1663), New Jersey (1664), and Pennsylvania (1682). The 13th colony, Georgia, formed in 1732.

Fast Fact

In 1638, Sweden established a colony called New Sweden in parts of today's Delaware, Pennsylvania, Maryland, and New Jersey. The Dutch captured it in 1655.

This map shows the early United States, which was formed from the 13 British colonies, not long after declaring independence.

Historians often divide the colonies into three regions. The New England Colonies were Connecticut, Massachusetts, New Hampshire, and Rhode Island. The Middle Colonies were Delaware, New Jersey, New York, and Pennsylvania. And the Southern Colonies were Maryland, North Carolina, South Carolina, Virginia, and Georgia.

Europeans moved to these colonies for many reasons. Some sought riches, such as gold, or economic opportunities, such as land to farm. Others wanted freedom to practice their religion, or belief system.

Some colonial governments offered rights that European governments didn't, but many rights didn't apply to all people equally. Certain groups, including enslaved Africans, Native Americans, and women

Native Americans had little power to stop Europeans from taking their lands. Many died from diseases introduced by Europeans too.

in general, had limited rights or no rights at all under colonial law.

Where Were the Women?

When Jamestown, the first successful British settlement in North America, was established in the early 17th century, no women were among the original settlers. Several women arrived in the years that followed. More than a decade later, dozens of young women were brought to the colony for the purpose of marrying the male colonists.

Fast Fact

As Europeans arrived in what they called the New World, they took ownership of lands that Native Americans had lived on for at least 23,000 years.

Later groups of settlers, such as the Pilgrims who established Plymouth in what is now Massachusetts, included women from the start. However, women remained a small part of the overall population of the British colonies for many years.

Many colonial women faced common experiences as members of a **culture** in which men had control over women's lives. However,

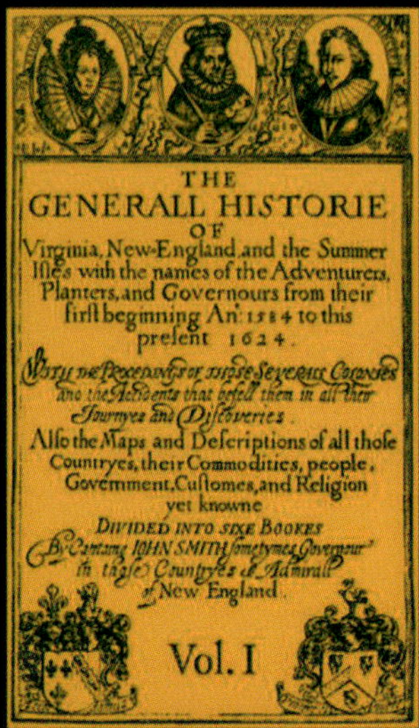

THE
GENERALL HISTORIE
OF
Virginia, New-England, and the Summer
Isles with the names of the Adventurers,
Planters, and Governours from their
first beginning An: 1584 to this
present 1624.
With the Proceedings of those Severall Colonies
and the Accidents that befell them in all their
Journyes and Discoveries.
Also the Maps and Descriptions of all those
Countryes, their Commodities, people,
Government, Customes, and Religion
yet knowne.
DIVIDED INTO SIXE BOOKES
By Captaine IOHN SMITH sometymes Governour
in those Countryes & Admirall
of New England.
Vol. I

THE NEW COLONISTS A.D. 1608.

Gent.

Thomas Graves.	Henry Collins.
Raleigh Chroshaw.	Hugh Wolleston.
Gabriel Beadle.	John Hoult.
John Beadle.	Thomas Norton.
John Russell.	George Yarington.
William Russell.	George Burton.
John Cuderington.	Thomas Abbay.
William Sambage.	William Dowman.
Henry Leigh.	Thomas Maxes.
Henry Philpot.	Michael Lowick.
Harmon Harrison.	Master Hunt.
Daniel Tucker.	Thomas Forrest.

John Dauxe.

Tradsmen.

Thomas Phelps.	Thomas Bradley.
John Prat.	John Burras. [III. 73.]
John Clarke.	Thomas Lavander.
Jeffrey Shortridge.	Henry Bell.
Dionis Oconor.	Master Powell.
Hugh Winne.	David Ellis.
David ap Hugh.	Thomas Gibson.

Labourers.

Thomas Dawse.	Williams.
Thomas Mallard.	Floud.
William Tayler.	Morley.
Thomas Fox.	Rose.
Nicholas Hancock.	Scot.
Walker.	Hardwyn.

Boyes.

Milman.	Hilliard.

Mistresse Forrest, and Anne Burras her maide; eight Dutch men and Poles, with some others, to the number of seaventie persons, &c.

151

Fast Fact

The first European women to arrive in the British colonies were Mistress Forrest, the wife of Thomas Forrest, and her maid, Anne Burras. They arrived in Jamestown in 1608, a year after the settlement was founded.

We know about Mistress Forrest and Anne Burras because of Captain John Smith's 1624 book *The Generall Historie of Virginia, New-England, and the Summer Isles.*

colonial women's lives could be different depending on several factors, such as their race, where they lived, their family's wealth and **livelihood**, and their background. For example, European women with wealth fared best, but most still were held back from achieving equal standing with men. European women with little wealth had fewer rights and opportunities. Enslaved women and Native American women often

NO PLACE FOR WOMEN?

Why did the Jamestown settlers not include women at first? Historian Alf J. Mapp Jr. reported, "It was thought that women had no place in the grim and often grisly [bloody] business of **subduing** a continent." Settlers recognized the risks, including conflicts with **Indigenous** populations who sometimes viewed the newcomers, not incorrectly, as dangerous. The first group prepared for women to arrive later to help populate the settlement. Edwin Sandys was the treasurer of the Virginia Company of London, whose ships carried settlers to Jamestown. In 1620, he said, "The plantation can never florish [flourish] till families be planted and the respect of wives and children fix the people on the soil."

This is a 20th-century illustration of the first large group of women who traveled to the Jamestown settlement from Europe.

faced the worst treatment. There were exceptions in every group, however. Some remarkable women left their mark on colonial history, despite considerable obstacles.

This map shows the land overseen by the Virginia Company of London as well as the location of Jamestown.

LAND GRANTED BY CHARTER TO THE VIRGINIA COMPANY IN 1609

THE FIRST YEARS

Chapter Two

At the time the British North American colonies were first established, European women lived in a patriarchal society. That means men had power over the home, the government, and society in general in most areas. Married women were under the control of their husbands. In British law, this control was called coverture. It meant that a married woman had no legal standing. So, she couldn't control property or money, even if she brought it into the marriage.

Fast Fact

Coverture didn't affect unmarried or widowed adult women. They could buy and sell property and take part in business and legal deals. Men still didn't view them as their equals, but they had more power.

What Happened at Jamestown

In Britain, women mainly took care of the domestic chores, or the work involved with the home, such as cooking, cleaning, and raising children. The men of early Jamestown didn't want to do this work, even though there weren't enough women to do it. They also

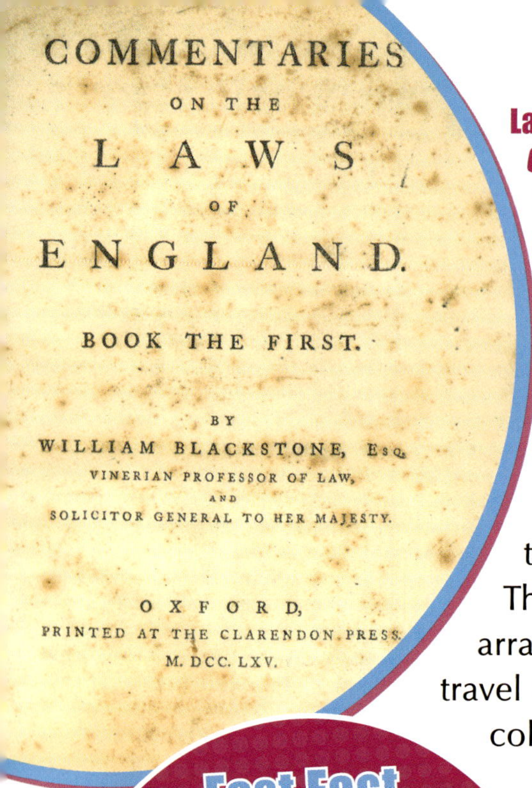
COMMENTARIES
ON THE
LAWS
OF
ENGLAND.
BOOK THE FIRST.
BY
WILLIAM BLACKSTONE, Esq.
VINERIAN PROFESSOR OF LAW,
AND
SOLICITOR GENERAL TO HER MAJESTY.
OXFORD,
PRINTED AT THE CLARENDON PRESS.
M. DCC. LXV.

Lawyer William Blackstone explained in his *Commentaries on the Laws of England* (published between 1765 and 1770) that husbands "covered" their wives under British law. They were one legal body after marriage.

didn't want to plant and care for the crops of the settlement because they observed Native American women doing it. This refusal to do what they believed was "women's work" made the settlement a difficult place to live.

The Virginia Company of London arranged for 90 unmarried women to travel to Jamestown in 1620 to marry male colonists. Company treasurer Edwin Sandys called them "younge [young], handsome and honestly educated maydes [maids]." The company hoped these marriages would produce families that would stabilize the colony, which wasn't certain to succeed. The next year, in 1621, 57 more women were sent to Jamestown.

Fast Fact

It's true that Native American women cared for crops, but many Native American peoples, including the Haudenosaunee (Iroquois) of the Northeast, had matriarchal societies. That means women held decision-making roles.

For many of these women, their daily work wasn't just in the house. They labored in the fields to keep the crops alive. Later laws would try to stop white women from working in the fields, so life in the colonies would mirror life in Britain, but early colonial communities were just trying to survive. Also, because colonial society wasn't the same as Europe, some women with wealth even rose to

Fast Fact

Some colonial women tried to exercise their limited freedom by speaking out in their community. However, a 1662 Virginia law allowed a wife who spoke against her husband or neighbors to be plunged underwater.

operate successful businesses. In the 1660s, Anne Toft, who was a single woman, traded with Dutch and British merchants and owned land in Virginia, Maryland, and the Caribbean island of Jamaica.

Enslaved Women

While some colonial women were exercising freedoms, others had liberty stripped away. Europeans enslaved African women, transported them to the colonies, and sold them to colonists. Some of the first enslaved workers were treated more like indentured servants, who were people who agreed to work, often years, in exchange for money or something

Europeans first transported enslaved Africans to Virginia in 1619. Colonists increasingly turned to enslaved people as a workforce rather than indentured servants. They could enslave them for their whole lives.

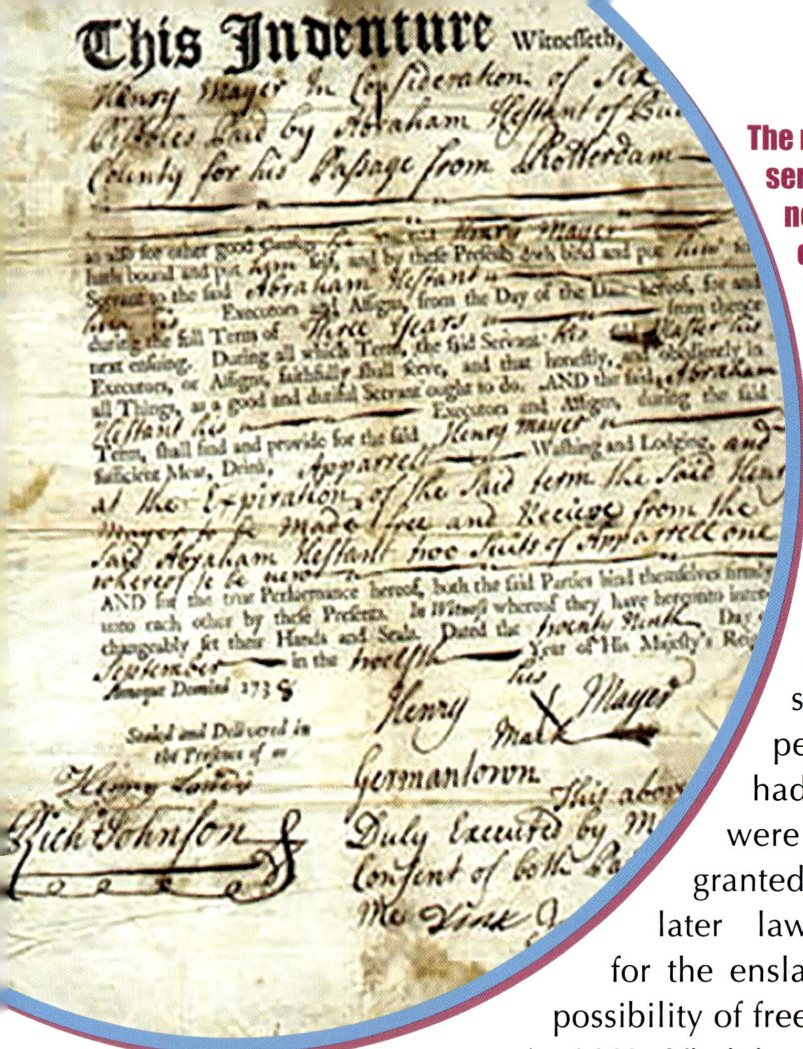

This Indenture Witnesseth,

The number of indentured servants didn't meet the need for workers, especially on farms in the South. Slavery became common. This image shows an indentured servant's contract with their employer.

else. Like colonial indentured servants, some early enslaved people in the colonies had a few rights and were sometimes even granted freedom. However, later laws removed rights for the enslaved and ended the possibility of freedom.

A 1662 Virginia law declared, "All children borne in this country shalbe [shall be] held bond or free only according to the condition of the mother," meaning that children born to free women were free and those born to enslaved women were forever bonded, or enslaved.

Not all Black women in the 13 colonies were enslaved. Even free Black women held few rights, however.

NATIVE AMERICAN WOMEN

Unlike European colonial society, many Native American groups held women as equals to men. Women held positions of leadership and respect. Their work within their community was as important to survival as men's work. Native American women had various relationships with the colonists. Some acted as guides and **translators** between colonists and Indigenous groups. Some married colonists and lived in white settlements. However, when colonists and Native Americans were in conflict, violence against Indigenous women was common. Colonists killed Native American women because they could bear children and increase the Native population. Colonists and explorers also enslaved thousands of Native American men and women.

Europeans sometimes sentenced Indigenous people to servitude for breaking colonial laws.

Colonial women were typically in charge of caring for the children in the colony, as shown in this image.

LIFE AND LIMITATIONS

Chapter Three

As the 17th century progressed, more successful settlements and colonies grew up along the coast. Women continued to move to the colonies, and those who were raised in the colonies usually married, had children, and kept their home in order. Some **defied** these expectations, but most had no choice. A lack of education was one factor that held them back from exploring other options.

Education

A woman's education depended on her family's background, including their wealth and where they lived. Some colonies had community schools where young girls attended along with boys, though girls were expected to learn less. The goal in the New England colonies was for girls to know how to read so they could read the Bible. However, school wasn't required by law, so many girls stayed home to help with chores. They grew up not knowing how to read.

Fast Fact

The Virginia colony had a female illiteracy rate of 70 percent at one point.

For many girls, their mothers were their teachers, and they learned their subjects at home. What they learned

Abigail Adams, the wife of John Adams and a First Lady of the United States, wrote letters that give us a glimpse into a woman's life in colonial New England. She wished she had had more education.

sometimes depended on the family's expectations for their daughters' future. Merchant families might teach their daughters math and **bookkeeping** skills, for example. Wealthy families might teach their daughters about art, dance, and music, as these were considered appropriate for upper-class women. Girls born into poverty might learn skills that had to do with keeping house and watching over the family farm, without learning to read or write.

Fast Fact

Some colonial women who learned to read and write kept diaries, helping historians learn directly from women what life was like for them.

AN EARLY SCHOOL FOR GIRLS

While most women had little formal education in the American colonies, there were exceptions. In 1742, Countess Benigna von Zinzendorf established in Pennsylvania perhaps the first school for girls in the colonies. It was called the Bethlehem Boarding School for Girls (later, the Moravian Female Seminary). It began as a kind of elementary school but became focused on higher education. Like many schools of the time, it taught religion—the Moravian Church of the Protestant faith—but also reading, writing, math, geography, history, astronomy, music, German, and English, as well as housekeeping skills such as sewing. The school maintained that "when you educate a woman, you educate an entire family."

Bethlehem Boarding School for Girls changed names many times. It became Moravian University in 2021, shown here. Its student body today includes both men and women.

It was even less likely that enslaved women would receive an education. Some colonies, including South Carolina, passed laws that made it illegal to teach enslaved people to read or write. Enslavers worried educated workers could run away more easily.

After Marriage

Many colonial women married at a young age, often as teenagers. After marriage, a woman was expected to have children because children could help on farms and in family businesses. However, giving birth

> **Fast Fact**
>
> Women faced great societal pressure to marry. In fact, communities and even their own families sometime shunned women who refused to marry.

during colonial times was full of danger for both mother and baby. Many women died giving birth because of an overall lack of medical knowledge, and more than half of all children born during this time died in their first few years of life. Still, despite the danger and heartache, colonial women were expected to keep having children.

Married women oversaw the household. If the family didn't have hired help or enslaved workers, the woman had to clean, cook, and care for the children. These chores were time-consuming. In colonial times, making a meal could take hours. Women prepared meals over a fire they also built and tended. Women might also make, mend, or wash clothes, care for livestock, make candles, or tend to their garden or farm.

If a woman married into a wealthy family, she might oversee enslaved workers who did the household work. Enslaved women truly had the hardest time of all. They did all the household work for their enslavers and then took care of their own children and living areas. Their work never ended, from sunup to sundown and sometimes longer.

This is a reconstruction of Christiana Campbell's Williamsburg tavern. She opened it in 1755 after her husband died.

CONSIDERABLE CONTRIBUTIONS

Chapter Four

While what was termed "women's work" was undoubtedly central to the survival of settlements in the 18th century, records show colonial women ran successful businesses too. For example, Christiana Campbell and Jane Vobe owned taverns in Williamsburg, Virginia, in the mid-1700s. Other women owned shops, had laundry businesses, and worked as **midwives**. Virginia midwife Catherine Blaikley delivered more than 3,000 babies in her career, according to a local newspaper.

Fast Fact

In Georgia, the last of the 13 British colonies established, the government granted land to white women and allowed them to purchase additional land. This was part of an effort to colonize the area. Some European women became large farm owners and enslavers.

Names to Know

Perhaps the most famous of the women featured in colonial history books is a Native American known today as Pocahontas, though she had several Native names. The daughter of a Powhatan chief, Pocahontas was born near the Jamestown settlement. She was

Pocahontas was a Powhatan woman who aided the settlers at Jamestown in Virginia, helping the colonists survive.

around 10 when the British first arrived. Colonial leader John Smith wrote that Pocahontas saved his life, though some doubt this story. However, her friendship with Smith and the colonists likely helped save them from starvation and other dangers. Pocahontas was later kidnapped by the British and married to colonist John Rolfe, forging a peace between the Powhatan and the colonists for a time.

This 1867 print shows an artist's idea of the wedding of Pocahontas and John Rolfe.

Anne Hutchinson, shown here on trial, is remembered as an early defender of women's rights.

Anne Hutchinson arrived in Boston in the Massachusetts Bay Colony in 1634. A **Puritan**, she began holding meetings for women to discuss religious ideas. Later, men joined the gatherings too. When Hutchinson questioned some Puritan ideas, male religious leaders acted against

Phillis Wheatley was freed from enslavement around 1774, but her life wasn't easy. She died in poverty in 1784.

her. They disliked that she, a woman, spoke with authority. She refused to back down. Hutchinson and her family were **banished** from the colony. They moved to Rhode Island and then to New Netherland (which became New York) where she was killed during an attack by Native Americans.

Fast Fact

Phillis Wheatley published her first book of poetry (and the only one published in her lifetime), *Poems on Various Subjects, Religious and Moral,* in 1773.

Phillis Wheatley was an enslaved African who defied the odds to become a respected writer. Born around 1753 in West Africa, she was captured when she was about 8 and enslaved. Traders sold her to John and Susanna Wheatley of Boston, Massachusetts. The Wheatleys encouraged Phillis to read and write, and later to become a poet. Some of her poetry was published in newspapers. One 1770 poem, *An Elegiac Poem, on the Death of the Celebrated Divine ... George Whitefield,* was printed throughout the colonies and made her famous.

BOYCOTTS AND SPINNING BEES

At the end of the 1760s, some American colonists tried to signal their disagreement with British rule with a **boycott** of British goods. For this action to work, women needed to take part. For example, an agreement in Boston, Massachusetts, in 1767 to ban British goods had 650 signatures, of which 55 were women's. Participating in a ban on British imports meant that many women had to make certain goods for the first time. Women's **ingenuity** shone. They held "spinning bees," events in which women would spin their own cotton and linen to fill the need for cloth for clothing.

Fast Fact

Penelope Barker of North Carolina held a tea party in 1774. Fifty women signed an agreement to boycott British cloth and tea, stating, "We ... will not promote ye [the] wear of any manufacturer from England until such time that all acts which tend to enslave our Native country shall be repealed."

War Approaches

In the second half of the 1700s, the American colonies began a power struggle with Great Britain. A war for independence broke out in 1775.

Women held important roles in the war effort. Many became head of their family, farms, and businesses as their husbands joined the military. Some became spies who put their lives in danger to gain enemy information. Others joined the action on the battlefield. In these ways and others, colonial women helped build a new nation and a brighter future for American women.

A TIMELINE OF COLONIAL WOMEN

1608
Women arrive in Jamestown, the first permanent British colonial settlement in North America.

1616
Captain John Smith reports that Pocahontas saved his life.

1619
The first enslaved people arrive near Jamestown.

1620
About 90 women arrive in Jamestown.

1637
Anne Hutchinson is banished from the Massachusetts Bay Colony.

1662
A Virginia law declares that children born to enslaved women are enslaved for life.

1755
Christiana Campbell opens a tavern in Williamsburg.

1767
Fifty-five women in Boston, Massachusetts, sign an agreement to boycott British goods.

1767
Phillis Wheatley publishes her first poem.

1775
The American Revolution begins, with women playing key roles in the war.

THINK ABOUT IT!

1. How could we learn more about certain women in colonial times?
2. Why do you think women agreed to travel to Jamestown to marry men they didn't know?
3. Why might Anne Hutchinson be viewed as an early women's rights hero?
4. Why do you think so few records of Native American women are included in early American history?

GLOSSARY

banish: To use authority to force someone to leave a place.

bookkeeping: Recording the actions and money dealings of a business.

boycott: The act of refusing to have dealings with a person or business to force change.

culture: The beliefs and ways of life of a group of people.

defy: To refuse to obey. Also, to resist.

illiteracy: Having to do with the inability to read or write.

Indigenous: Describing the earliest known inhabitants of a place.

ingenuity: Skill or cleverness at figuring something out.

livelihood: How someone supports themselves economically.

midwife: One whose job is to help women and children during birth.

Puritan: A member of a Protestant religious group in England and New England that opposed many practices of the Church of England.

repeal: To do away with.

shun: To avoid someone or something on purpose.

subdue: To bring under control.

translator: One who tells what words in one language mean in another.

FIND OUT MORE

Books

Collison, Campbell. *The 13 Original Colonies*. Minneapolis, MN: Bearport Publishing, 2021.

Doyle, Abby Badach. *Pocahontas*. New York, NY: Enslow Publishing, 2023.

Miller, Brandon Marie. *Women of Colonial America: 13 Stories of Courage and Survival in the New World*. Chicago, IL: Chicago Review Press, 2022.

Websites

Colonial Era

www.womenshistory.org/education-resources/topics/colonial-era
Read more about specific women of the colonial period on this site from the National Women's History Museum.

Daily Life in Colonial America

www.worldhistory.org/article/1722/daily-life-in-colonial-america/
Learn more about what life was like in the 13 colonies from the World History Encyclopedia.

Women in Colonial Virginia

encyclopediavirginia.org/entries/women-in-colonial-virginia/
Check out this detailed source from Encyclopedia Virginia.

Publisher's note to educators and parents: Our editors have carefully reviewed these websites to ensure that they are suitable for students. Many websites change frequently, however, and we cannot guarantee that a site's future contents will continue to meet our high standards of quality and educational value. Be advised that students should be closely supervised whenever they access the internet.

INDEX